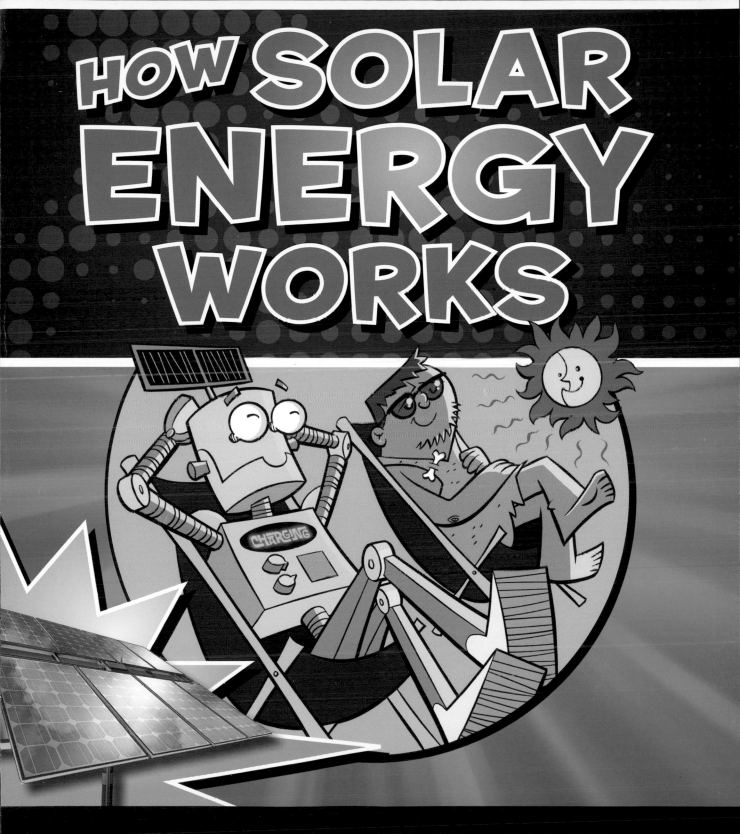

HOW SOLAR ENERGY WORKS

BY JENNIFER SWANSON • ILLUSTRATED BY GLEN MULLALY

Published by The Child's World®
980 Lookout Drive • Mankato, MN 56003-1705
800-599-READ • www.childsworld.com

ACKNOWLEDGMENTS
The Child's World®: Mary Berendes, Publishing Director
Content Consultant: Paul Ohmann, PhD, Associate Professor
 of Physics, University of St. Thomas
The Design Lab: Design and production
Red Line Editorial: Editorial direction

LIBRARY OF CONGRESS
CATALOGING-IN-PUBLICATION DATA
Swanson, Jennifer.
How solar energy works / by Jennifer Swanson; illustrated
by Glen Mullaly.
      p. cm.
Includes bibliographical references and index.
ISBN 978-1-60973-221-9 (library reinforced : alk. paper)
. Solar energy—Juvenile literature. I. Mullaly, Glen, 1968– ill.
I. Title.
TJ810.3.S93 2011
621.47—dc23   2011013785

Photo Credits © Krzysztof Krzyscin/iStockphoto, cover, 1;
John Kroetch/iStockphoto, 6; Elena Elisseeva/iStockphoto,
9; Baris Simsek/iStockphoto, 12; HultonArchive/iStockphoto,
20; Nataliia Fedori/iStockphoto, 21; NASA Headquarters/
Greatest Images of NASA (NASA-HQ-GRIN), 22 (left);
Michael Fuery/iStockphoto, 22 (right); Katrin Solansky/
iStockphoto, 23 (left); Nakisa Photo/iStockphoto, 23
(right); David Hill/iStockphoto, 25; Iñigo Quintanilla Gomez/
iStockphoto, 26; Jim Pruitt/iStockphoto, 28; Doug Berry/
iStockphoto, 30

Printed in the United States of America in Mankato,
Minnesota.
July 2011
PA02092

ABOUT THE AUTHOR
Jennifer Swanson's first love is science,
and she is thrilled to be able to combine
that with her passion for writing. She has
a bachelor of science in chemistry from
the US Naval Academy and a master
of science in education from Walden
University. Jennifer is currently employed
as a middle school science instructor for
Johns Hopkins University's Center for
Talented Youth.

ABOUT THE ILLUSTRATOR
Glen Mullaly draws neato pictures for kids
of all ages from his swanky studio on the
west coast of Canada. He lives with his
awesomely understanding wife and their
spectacularly indifferent cat. Glen loves
old books, magazines, and cartoons, and
someday wants to illustrate a book on How
Monsters Work!

TABLE OF CONTENTS

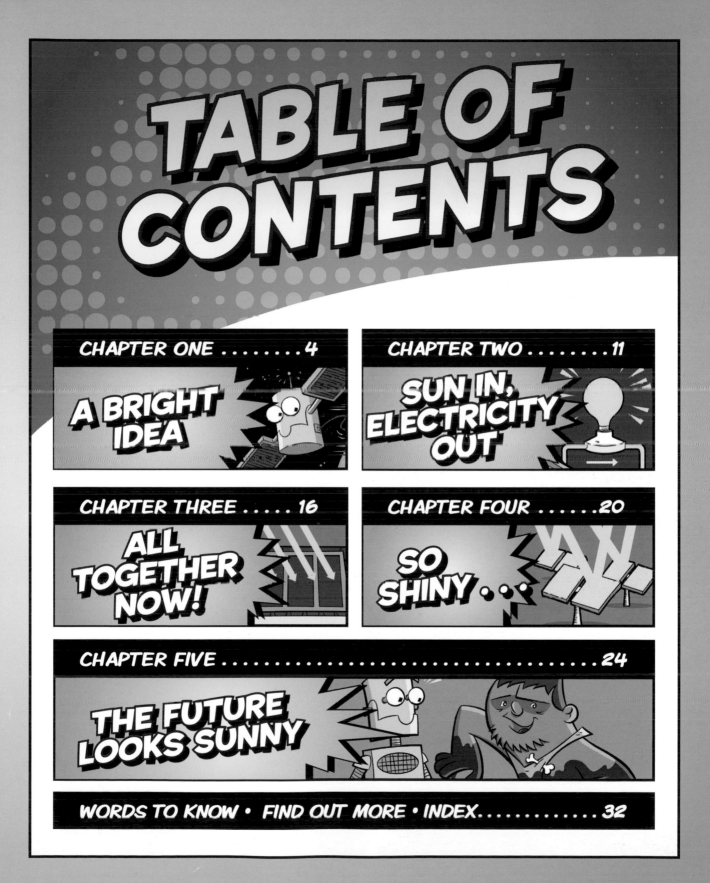

CHAPTER ONE

A BRIGHT IDEA

It's a hot day, but you're shivering at your desk. The air conditioner in your classroom is blasting right on you. You can practically see your breath. What a waste of energy!

The bell rings and you run outside. You turn your face to the sky. Ahhhhh. The sun's rays are doing their job. They are bringing energy to keep you warm.

It's something we all take for granted, this giant ball in the sky. Did you know that one hour of sunshine has enough energy to power the entire planet for a whole year? Wow!

Energy from the sun is called solar energy. And it comes with a special challenge. It's just way too spread out. How can we collect the sun's rays? How can we

make the sun's power useful? People have been trying
to find answers to those questions for thousands of
years. Let's take a quick look back at the history of
solar power.

The first usable **solar cell** was developed by US scientists. This device used energy from the sun to make electricity. This was a huge step, but it had a major drawback—price. It cost about 600 times as much as regular electricity. So, solar energy was used only to power small electronics, such as radios and toys.

A solar-powered calculator

A French scientist developed the first solar-powered steam engine. Later, he connected it to a refrigeration device. He used his invention to freeze a block of ice, creating a solar ice cube.

According to legend, Archimedes, a famous Greek scientist, used bronze shields to focus the sun's rays on a wooden ship. This caused the Roman ship to burn, saving Greece from attack. Other people used glass and metals to focus the sun's rays.

Solar power is on the rise. Rooftop panels make electricity for homes. Solar "farms" with hundreds of giant mirrors power entire cities. The sun's rays are powering spacecraft, calculators, watches, and TVs. Scientists are even working on cars that run on sunshine. Imagine riding in a car that doesn't need gas!

Solar power has two huge benefits. It won't run out (at least not for billions of years). And it doesn't harm Earth. The main problem is that solar equipment is expensive. But as the technology gets better, costs are coming down.

Money saved by switching to solar powered electricity in a typical US house: an average of $73 per month

Cost of setting up a complete solar electric system in a typical US house: from $12,500 to $30,000

Number of years a solar panel lasts: 20–25 years

Number of US solar "farms" at end of 2008: 11

Percentage of US energy provided by solar power in 2009: 1

THE POWER OF SUNSHINE

Just how big is the sun? Think of it this way: If Earth weighed as much as a hamster, the sun would weigh as much as two elephants. Wow!

This huge glowing ball holds an incredible amount of energy. That energy travels to Earth in the form of light—the fastest thing in the universe. It makes the 93 million-mile trip in just 8 minutes and 20 seconds!

Pretty much every power resource on Earth comes from the sun. Sun causes trees to grow, making wood for fires. It gave life to ancient plants and animals. Then, over millions of years, they turned into natural gas, oil, and coal. Sun causes the wind that spins windmills. It causes the rushing water that drives hydroelectric power plants.

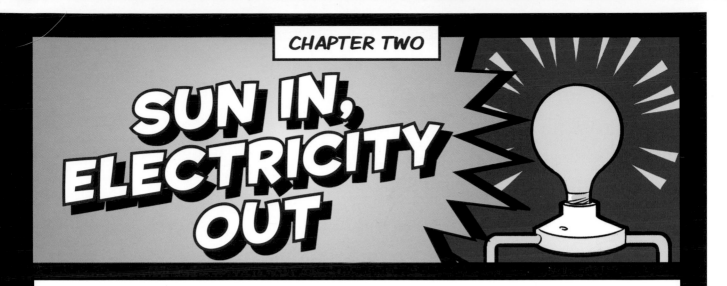

CHAPTER TWO

SUN IN, ELECTRICITY OUT

A solar cell is a device that changes the sun's energy into electricity. It can be as small as a penny, as wide as a small book, or any size in between. One cell doesn't make a lot of power. So, many are linked together. About 40 cells make up one solar panel. Then the solar panels are connected and placed on roofs to power a building.

Inside a solar cell are two very thin sheets of **silicon**. Silicon is everywhere on Earth—it's the main ingredient in sand. It's also a **semiconductor**.

> Look what I made. A solar panel!

That means we can control the flow of electricity across it.

Antsy Electrons

Like all matter, silicon is made up of tiny particles called atoms. Atoms can be seen only by the world's most powerful microscopes. They are the most basic

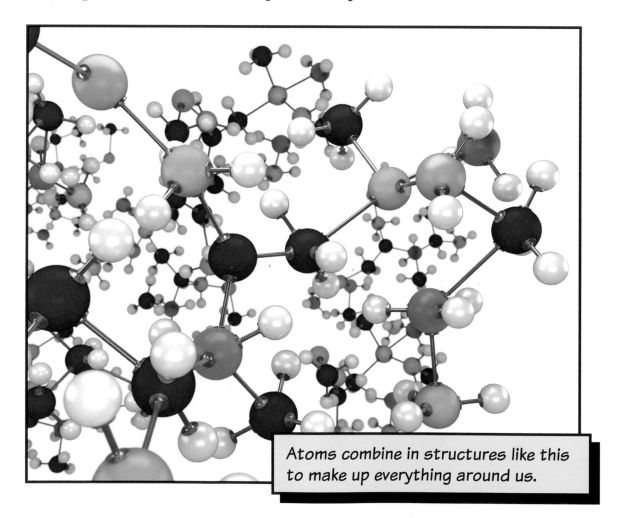

Atoms combine in structures like this to make up everything around us.

units of matter. Only about 100 kinds of atoms combine to make everything in the universe, from Jupiter to rubber bands to you.

Each tiny atom contains even smaller parts, called **electrons**. Electrons spin around inside an atom. Sometimes atoms get excited, and electrons break free. This makes electricity. Think about it—*elec*tron . . . *elec*tricity. Electricity is just electrons on the loose. Keep that in mind as we return to solar cells.

Back to Business

To make a solar cell, silicon is heated to super high temperatures. Then it is formed into very thin sheets. Special chemicals are added to the sheets. These chemicals make the electrons in the silicon atoms kind of antsy. The electrons are ready to get going at the slightest shove.

That's where sunlight comes in. Sunlight shoves those electrons. It makes them break away, generating electricity in a solar cell.

Let's take a closer look.

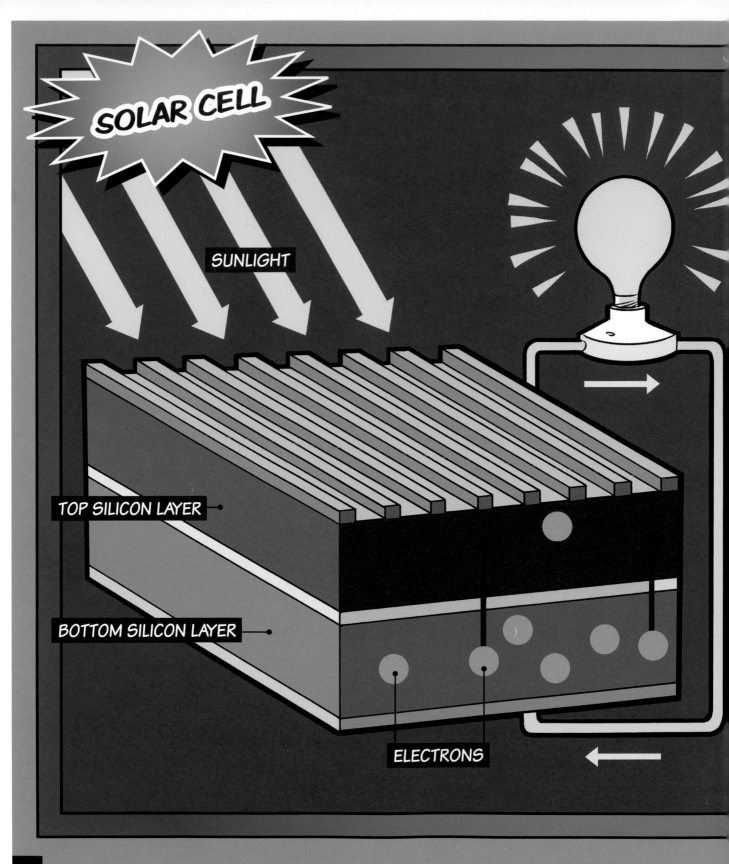

SOLAR CELL

SUNLIGHT

TOP SILICON LAYER

BOTTOM SILICON LAYER

ELECTRONS

1. Remember that silicon is a semiconductor. We can control the flow of electrons inside it. And flowing electrons equals electricity. A solar cell has two silicon layers. The bottom layer has a region of extra electrons. The top layer has a region with quite a bit fewer.

2. Sunlight comes in through the top. It knocks off a few electrons in the bottom layer. These electrons flow to the top layer.

3. As the sun beats down, a steady stream of electrons flows from the top layer. This makes an electric current. The electricity flows out of the solar cell to charge batteries, turn on lights, and do whatever else is needed around the house.

4. After they've done their work, the electrons flow all the way back to the bottom layer. The process starts all over again.

LET'S BE LAZY

Sometimes, the sun's energy is used without a solar cell or any other device. This is called passive solar power. Think of an outdoor swimming pool that doesn't have an electric heater. Instead, the sun's rays warm the water. No extra equipment is needed. Can you think of ways you use passive solar power?

CHAPTER THREE

ALL TOGETHER NOW!

So, now you know how a single solar cell works. You know that solar cells combine to make solar panels. The next step is to get those solar panels up on a roof. How does that work? Often, a house with solar panels is still connected to the **power grid**. The house makes a lot of its own electricity. But those solar panels need sunshine to work. The homeowners still rely on the electric company for backup power on cloudy or dark days.

In the following example, the house is not connected to the power grid. It uses a battery for backup. The battery stores electricity created by the solar panels. Let's take a closer look.

1. Energy from the sun hits the solar panels and creates electricity.

2. Electricity goes through a charge controller. This device lets the battery recharge only when it needs to. This makes the battery last longer.

3. Electricity that is not needed right away is stored in the battery for later use.

4. Electricity that is needed right away goes to the inverter. This changes the electricity into a form the house can use.

4 INVERTER

CHAPTER FOUR

SO SHINY...

Solar panels on a house turn sunshine directly into electricity. But solar power works differently at a solar farm, or solar thermal power plant. There are no solar cells. Instead, special mirrors focus the sun's rays. This creates heat. Then the heat boils water to make steam. Steam spins a turbine in a **generator**, where electricity is made.

A solar thermal plant can have hundreds of mirrors sticking up from the ground, enough to generate power for hundreds of houses.

TIME LINE

AROUND 200 BC
Archimedes uses bronze shields to burn Roman ships.

1200 AD
Ancestors of the Pueblo Indians design their homes to capture the winter sun.

1767
A Swiss scientist builds the very first solar energy collector.

1830s
A solar energy collector is used to cook food in Africa.

1839
Alexandre Edmond Becquerel discovers that sunlight can be used to make electricity.

1860–1880
French scientist August Mouchet develops and experiments with solar-powered steam engines.

1883
American inventor Charles Fritts describes the first solar cell.

1954
Scientists at Bell Telephone Laboratories invent the first solar cell that can create a useful amount of electricity.

HOW A SOLAR FARM WORKS

1. The giant mirrors are controlled by computers at a central station. As the sun moves overhead, the mirrors tilt to reflect the most sunlight.

2. The mirrors direct the sunlight toward a receiving tower. The tower has a tank with fluid inside. The energy from the mirrors heats up this fluid.

3. The heated fluid travels down a pipe from the top of the tower. It flows to another tank that has water.

1964
NASA launches Nimbus, a satellite that is powered by solar cells.

1970s
The cost of solar power is going down. It is now being used for railroad-crossing signs, lighthouse lights, and some other public projects.

1973
"Solar One" is built by the University of Delaware. This house uses solar power during the day and electricity from a power plant at night.

6. The flowing electrons create an electric current. It is sent over wires into the city.

5. The steam spins a turbine, or wheels, in a generator. This causes the generator's magnets to spin, sending electrons flowing into nearby wires.

4. The hot fluid turns the water into steam.

1981
The first solar-powered aircraft is flown across the English Channel.

1983
A home in eastern New York is the first to run completely on solar power.

1993
In California, the first solar power system to send energy to multiple homes is installed.

2010
California officials commit to building what will be the world's largest solar power plant.

CHAPTER FIVE

THE FUTURE LOOKS SUNNY

Solar energy has so many benefits. Here are the top three:

1. It's renewable. There's plenty of sunshine, and it will not run out for billions of years.
2. It's clean. Using solar power creates barely any pollution.
3. It's everywhere. We don't have to buy sunlight from foreign countries.

What's the Hold Up?

So, why doesn't everyone use solar energy? The big drawback is cost. Sure, sunlight is free. But solar equipment is not.

This modern office building runs on solar power.

The cost of switching to solar power depends on a lot of things. How much electricity you use is key. Another big factor is how sunny your area is. People living in sunny states need a lot fewer panels. Also, government

Mirrors at a solar farm reflect light onto a receiving tower.

tax programs and rebates from the electric company can bring down the cost by as much as 75 percent. But again, that exact amount depends on where you live. Given all these factors, the cost of setting up a complete solar electric system ranges from $12,500 to more than $30,000 in a single house. That's a lot of cash!

But why are solar panels so expensive, anyway? One reason has to do with how well they work. As of 2011, solar panels are able to use only about one-fifth of the sunlight they absorb.

But scientists are working hard to find new and better ways to harness the sun's energy. And they are making huge strides. Maybe by the time you read this book fewer solar panels will be needed to do the same job as before. That means costs are going down.

SUNLIGHT FOR RENT

In some states, a cheaper option is available. Homeowners can rent solar panels instead of buying them. They pay the renting company to get all set up. Then they pay a fee for each month of service. If there is a problem, they just call the company to fix it.

What's Next?

What might a new, improved solar panel look like? It may still use silicon sheets. But a new, better coating would trap more sunlight.

Another idea involves a special paint made of carbon **nanotubes**. Each of these tiny tubes is 50,000 times thinner than a human hair. The tubes can change sunlight to electricity, just like silicon.

Homeowners could use this amazing black paint to make their own solar cells. They'd slap it on a special sheet of plastic. Or they might even print out the solar cells on an inkjet printer. Then they'd hang their homemade solar cells on the roof, a wall, or any sunny spot to make their own power stations.

A *scientist working on-site to research solar technology*

Right now the technology is way out of the average person's price range. And scientists still have more work to do. But the promise is huge. Those tiny tubes trap almost all the sunlight that hits them. Plus, they can be used to actually concentrate the sun's energy. Scientists are experimenting with nanotube cells that are 100 times more powerful than what's out there now. Amazing!

The future of solar power depends on lots of hard work and bright ideas, but we're getting there. Who knows where the sun's energy will take us?

Have you ever seen those big mounds of dirt covering a huge trash pile? The land there isn't good for growing much of anything. In fact, all that rotting garbage can smell pretty bad.

What if we could find a way to turn that garbage into electricity? Scientists are doing just that. They have come up with a special green tarp that lies on top of a garbage dump. The tarp is covered with thin solar panels to capture the sun's energy. At the same time, it collects the gas given off from the rotting garbage and turns that into energy. One garbage heap outside of Atlanta, Georgia, is expected to produce enough energy to power 150 houses.

Look at all this wasted electricity!

WORDS TO KNOW

electrons (ih-LEK-trons): Electrons are the parts of atoms that spin around the centers. Electricity is the flow of electrons from one place to another.

generator (JEN-uh-ray-tuhr): A generator is the part of a power plant where electricity is generated. Inside a generator, electricity is made by magnets spinning inside coils of copper wire.

nanotubes (NAN-oh-toobz): Nanotubes are microscopic tube-like structures. Scientists are experimenting with carbon nanotubes to make solar cells of the future.

power grid (POW-uhr GRID): A power grid is a system of cables used to send electric power throughout a region. Homeowners with solar panels often rely on electricity from the power grid for backup.

semiconductor (sehm-ee-kuhn-DUK-tuhr): A semiconductor is a substance that can be used to generate electricity in a solar cell. Silicon is a semiconductor.

silicon (SIHL-uh-kuhn): Silicon is a common substance found on Earth. Silicon is used in solar cells to convert sunlight to electricity.

solar cell (SOH-luhr SEHL): A solar cell is a device that converts sunlight to electricity. A solar cell connects to other solar cells to make a solar panel.

FIND OUT MORE

Visit our Web site for links about how solar energy works: *childsworld.com/links*

Note to Parents, Teachers, and Librarians: We routinely verify our Web links to make sure they are safe and active sites. So encourage your readers to check them out!

INDEX